Birdhouse

by

ANNA WOODFORD

SALT

LONDON

PUBLISHED BY SALT PUBLISHING
Dutch House, 307–308 High Holborn, London WC1V 7LL United Kingdom

© Anna Woodford, 2010

The right of Anna Woodford to be identified as the
author of this work has been asserted by her in accordance
with Section 77 of the Copyright, Designs and Patents Act 1988.

Salt Publishing 2010

Printed and bound in Great Britain by
CPI Antony Rowe, Chippenham and Eastbourne

Typeset in Swift 9.5 / 13

ISBN 978 1 84471 788 0 paperback

1 3 5 7 9 8 6 4 2

Birdhouse

ANNA WOODFORD's pamphlet *Party Piece* was a winner in the
Poetry Business Competition. Her pamphlet *Trailer* was a Poetry
Book Society Choice. She has received an Eric Gregory Award, a
major Leverhulme Award, an Arvon/Jerwood Apprenticeship, a
Hawthornden Fellowship and a residency at the Blue Mountain
Center (New York). She has a PhD on the poetry of Sharon Olds
from Newcastle University. Her poetry commissions include
residencies at the Tyne & Wear Fire Service, Alnwick Garden
and Durham Cathedral.

Also by Anna Woodford

PAMPHLETS
Party Piece (Smith/Doorstop 2009)
Trailer (Five Leaves 2007)
The Higgins' Honeymoon (Driftwood 2001)

for Geoff and Archie

Contents

Acknowledgements

Acknowledgments are due to the following: *Acknowledged Land* [online], 14, *Diamond Twig* [online], *Horizon Review* [online], *Magma*, *Mslexia*, *New Writers' Magazine*, *North*, *The Poem* [online], *Poetry Ireland Review*, *Poetry Wales*, *The Reader*, *The Reater*, *Rialto*, the *SHOp*, *Times Literary Supplement*, *Tower Poetry* [online] and *The Wolf*.

Some of these poems first appeared in the anthologies *Gift* (University of Newcastle 2009), *The Body and the Book: Writings on Poetry and Sexuality* (Editions Rodopi B.V., 2008), *Ten Years of the Northern Writers' Awards* (New Writing North 2008), *Gategate* (The Northern Writers' Centre 2007), *Magnetic North* (New Writing North 2005) and the CD *Words From The Garden* (cawrecords 2007).

A selection of these poems also appeared in the pamphlets *Party Piece* (Smith/ Doorstop 2009), *Trailer* (Five Leaves 2007) and *The Higgins' Honeymoon* (Driftwood 2001). *Party Piece* was a winner in the international Poetry Business Competition, judged by Michael Longley. *Trailer* was a Poetry Book Society Choice.

Some of these poems were written as commissions for the Tyne & Wear Fire & Rescue Service, Alnwick Garden and Durham Cathedral.

The author would like to thank: the Leverhulme Trust for an artist in residence award, the Society of Authors for an Eric Gregory Award, the Arvon and Jerwood Foundations for an apprenticeship and New Writing North for a Northern Promise Award.

The author is grateful for a Hawthornden Fellowship and residencies at the Tyrone Guthrie Centre, Ireland and Blue Mountain Center, USA.

Birdhouse

You fiddle with the catch
between my legs until my mouth
springs open and I am
crowing like an everyday bird that has
entered the heights of an aviary. I am
scaling the bars, wide-
spreading my common or garden
fan while your beady eye hangs
over my body. My voice goes
flying in our feathered bed from
your forefinger and thumb, my next cry
rests on the tip of your tongue.

Epithalamium

I will stand at the foot of the umpteen steps
to the church among the mucky doves,
I will bring your letters, shredded into confetti,
when the bells spill over with your joy, with your joy,
I will wrap my arms around myself
and dance: no one will mind me
when your bride comes down the steps.
The sky will fall in after her like a train.

Trying

You are trying to be a father,
rubbing my breast's beauty spot,
I arch my back for a girl,
baby-cries escape my mouth.

We are months, maybe years
ahead of the midwife
who will pull the child out
of her sack like a rabbit.

All night you sleep foetal in my arms,
your body just within reach, just
out of reach.
I am beginning to dream

daily now, of a room full of globes
lit up and spinning
and a cot that can hardly contain
its enormity. One morning

I will slip out of bed, into that room.
Everything in the old world
will have inched over.
Our child will be breathing.

Desk

Dad raised his hand. The gavel fell.
   The following week the delivery man
left no stair uncursed
   as he dragged the desk like a cross
to my room. It was stuck
  by the dressing table, catching my hip
 when I danced in the mirror.
    It wasn't a dog or a TV,
it was a leg-up with the La Sagesse entrance exam,
a short step from there to university.

It was laden with trifles and pellucid jellies
  when I started to write. I saw myself
crowned with leaves in the reflected glory
   of the bay that overlooked
all the fences. There was a room
—a whole wing—of my parents' house
that they hadn't discovered. I entered
  through the desk like a wardrobe.
Mum sneaked in after me, cleaning up
     poems like snow from my floor.

Sex Education

Sister Ancilla bangs a ruler
at the trembling projector screen,
where four naked girls stand up in themselves.
They have come to walk us through puberty,
beginning with the baby steps of the youngest,
who trails behind a bigger sister.
Next, a teenager takes our place in this line-up,
caught with her pants down, she doesn't giggle or fidget.
Finally, the head girl is a fully rounded figure:
she is ready to break into a run, to bump into a man.

Sister Ancilla holds her ruler
and won't let it drop.
She turns to look for a volunteer:
'Which girl will tell me what's happening here?'

Relic

You pulled back from the other girls
    and laid a hand on my arm,
      touching me utterly.

Though I was beyond my mother and teachers
    and the educational psychologist
  had referred me, you

lifted me out of the High Church Of My Misery
    and set me down among the other girls
      in shopping centres and cinemas:
  in the playground I had run away from too early.

    I held on to your hand
      with its friendship bracelet
    and glittering nail polish
      long after you had gone.

    I carried the loss
      of your hand in my heart
    when I should have been unbuttoning
      my body and running after you
        into the open air.

The Goldilocks Variable

Some fairytales say she jumped
out of the window and ran home to her mother,
never to stray ever after.

Some say she came round to the idea
that her prince wouldn't come and settled
for shared living with the bears.

An Internet site describes her turning
into a glamour model called Goldie
who likes a good hiding

or, maybe, she's not out of the woods yet
and her hair went white,
slim-picking through the neighbourhood bins.

In Prague, an astronomer saw a light in the sky
and christened it for her
—and his mystery blonde girlfriend—

The Goldilocks Variable. It is an elusive star.
It isn't always shining. Sometimes it appears
to have vanished from the night's curtain-call.

Assembly

Newcastle. 1984. I am still in my chair
at assembly. Miss Murter is repeating
her command then pulling the chair
from under me so hard
that it is knocked off its feet
and falls to the floor
like a small, wooden child.

Murter's hand follows — raised
above the infants like
a bearded god — it swoops
then stops, as if
to gather itself, swoops and hits me
and hits me into
the middle of next week.

I am inconsolable, while Murter is
crossing herself, shouting out grace
in the stopped hall
of my head, where I hold her
— years later, I served my old teacher
coffee and she unbent over a cup
and patted my hand warmly.

Journey 14/35

Her father was driving
   not to the doctor's
for all her screaming
   but to school.

Between Sister Mary
   and the classroom
she found a way out
   by the bins.

Leaving other girls to get ahead
of her in History, she ran
into the real world
   without sitting the exam.

Going places, twenty odd years
   down the road,
I would give that girl a glimpse
of her future

if I could,
I would offer her a lift
to let her know
   that she's on her way somewhere.

Two Up Two Down

In a terrace house in Murton,
a bust of Beethoven is arranged
in a living room window.
Behind drawn curtains,
Annie is letting down a miniskirt,
Jack is looking through the *Echo*:
holes are cut in Christine Keeler's story.

Upstairs, Pat kicks out at Moira
as Annie uncovers a fresh row of daisies.
Moira rolls over murmuring
of her new skirt from Binns. It is nineteen-sixty-three.
In Murton it is earlier. Annie checks the hem
of her bairn's modesty. I will be born
over her dead body.

The Higgins' Honeymoon

The whole house cries out for a mistress,
bells emptying down catwalk corridors.
Eliza takes up two thirds of a mattress.
Henry's spare change collects in the ashtray,
none of the money he's thrown has stuck.
She's loud as a headboard,
slips into her comfortable mother tongue.
He whispers aitches into her ear,
rubs her breast's blind eye,
no lady comes. He rubs his head instead.
In Spain, it continues to rain.

Looking Back

If I could
I'd go back
and slide my tongue
out your mouth.
I'd pick up a tissue
and mop my damp praise
from your neck and your chest.
I'd take my pound of flesh
back. If there was a master tape
of our night
I'd get my hands on a copy
and set it to rewind,
so I could watch our bodies
unmaking love,
remaking the bed.
I'd leave nothing to chance.
I'd backtrack us all the way
out the bedroom
and into the lounge
and I wouldn't pause there
to pick up my coffee.

Guernica

We wandered around the Spanish gallery
which had been converted from a hospital
after the war. Pictures occupied the space
left by bodies. We weren't getting on,
nothing was new under the sun.
I didn't see the horse coming.
It charged down the wall and into my head,
battling with the spear in its side,
the stones of paint hurled at its body.

Back on home territory,
I cut the picture to size and
propped it above our dwindling fire
(the landlord didn't allow us to
hang up anything permanently).
On the night you left,
the horse's wound looked raw,
I reached out to touch it as though the paint
would come away wet beneath my fingers.

Big Bed Scene

My life falls open
at this page, it is
the definitive description
of you and me
having sex. Your body
has turned to cliché
in my hands, an editor would ring
my nipple's purple prose
but we were great
together, the way
I remember it.
Every time I look back
we're getting better with age.

Singing in the Bath

I am wearing the bath water.
My bare breasts are perfectly
suited to my bare body. A flash
of coarse hair is fitting
between my thighs. Only my nails
are polished on my nude
figure which is drifting
indecently into the morning. It is running
late. I need to stop
gazing into my navel. I need to start
covering my back. On the other hand,
which squeezes out a little soft soap,
I am up to my neck in hot water already.
How can I keep from singing?

Six Weeks

You swallowed the pills then walked as far as you could
away down the hospital corridor. The nurse kept your bed
 knowing sickness would overtake you.
 Soon you were a good girl throwing up
into a cardboard dish. The same as all the other hidden women
 on the ward, contracting behind cubicle curtains.

It was six weeks since you'd fallen.
 You were in trouble when you told me about him
on the morning after. Water was dripping
   through the holes in our living room ceiling.
We gathered pans and bowls and cups and egg-cups
   trying to contain the flood before the ceiling fell in.

Party Piece

My mother is taking a turn
   in my killer heels
—they could topple her—
      the old idol of her body
sways like a Madonna
      shouldered out of a Spanish cathedral.
 She breaks into a song,
            the crown of her voice
   slipped after wine and years
    at the centre of this living room:
 it is my brother's living room
  this new year, and my mother
is getting carried away. I raise a glass
  at her gathering. Now I can't hold her
  back or follow her.

Taking in the Washing

Next to your boxers, my bra
is undone, how vividly
it flowers, secured by your hand
and attended by the weather
of this everyday morning after.
When I think of my endless twenties — bras
drying slowly in single rooms — and now,
how everything has come out in the wash,
I cling to our line's unbrokenness:
it extends into our future
and past, at the far end Gran is
dolly-pegging Dad's nappies.

Going Underground

Two generations ago she went to war
with the Aunts in Bracknell and the girls at college,
who would have sniggered at her with her uptight bun,
joining forces with a Jewish Austrian.

Five foot of him, like the snapped
branch of a family tree, scar exposed
where he'd been torn from parents, cousins . . .
(freighted away like so much dead wood)
on different trains than the one which brought him to
    Nottingham, to her.

She unwrapped the rest of his life like a boiled sweet from
    her handbag,
removed his name—the German name that meant
he couldn't open doors for her—
called him Richard, name for a man she might have
    married.

Between Buckhurst Hill and Roding Valley,
she found their surname on the London Tube map—
Woodford—because she liked its sound. It was something
to pass on to the baby with Slovak eyes,
who didn't know his limbs had been broken,
who didn't know how far he'd come
—from the condemned line of men and women—
via the Central Line.

Darling

I was nobody's darling,
everybody's pet,
except when Gran came up,
I was her duck.
Darling was for girls who weren't
that special. They were the non-speaking angels
in the nativity. Their sandwiches cut into right angles,
their mothers ranging from affection to affectation
when they called them home
across the playground: 'Darling!'

Your mouth sums me up,
moving silently down my stomach,
singling out a thigh
but when you call me darling,
it's my mother's tongue in my head
that hushes you. I know it's only a word.
I knew as a back street driver at seven,
my eyes screwing streetlights into stars,
that when we passed the sign for Darlington,
it wouldn't live up to its promise.

Gran's Diary

All year December was coming
in your diary but you were taking it
one day at a time: an arboretum walk
on 6 January, later that month it was
Herbert's funeral. On 10 February:
a talk on the crisis in music was followed
by the gas-man after 12. All March,
though December was becoming inevitable,
you were making other plans: putting lunch with Marge
before the nurse; seeing the doctor and
The Gondoliers. It was 1999, people were talking
about the end of the world but you were counting
on another year: working out
the church cleaning rota into the Millennium; working out
your savings on three rainy days in April.
A week's holiday, from 20 August, was ruled out
by the consultant then, after a hospital scan,
it was the end of Summer Time, the year's last quarter.
Your remaining days are mainly blanks:
the word 'mnemonic'
underlined, a book reference and my name
on 19 November with a question mark beside it.
A couple of weeks later, my name is ringed,
red-lettered but this time you didn't make it.
Our arrangement then
is to meet again. You would have laughed
and said: 'Go on with you.' You were in heaven,
I was in December, where—
according to your diary—death was no more scary
than a visit to the dentist
followed by the Clarendon Christmas Party.

Gran's Parting Shot

The Eiffel Tower is raised
in the photo like a tour guide's
rolled umbrella. Beside it
Gran is blinking. Her husband
stepped back to compose
his little woman. She was
beyond his reach then. Her eyes
are shuttering. The strands of her bun
are unravelling like a sticky
French pastry. He should have
dropped his camera and held
her hand for longer. I could live
without this photo. It doesn't do
Gran justice but the Eiffel Tower
is still standing in her shadow.

Gran's Death

Only the blessed die in church.
You stumbled over your reading,
lost your place,

slipped through the choir ladies' fingers
and into God's hands.

I imagine you, on the other side,
repositioning your reading glasses,
talking over His answer.

Your husband is crying
into the wilderness of my ear,
but my sympathies (as they say
on the cards) are with you

and the Lord is with you
(as they say in the service) once
Dot and Rita can find words.

All boxed off. You called,
He answered.

And in front of the neighbours
with his heart on his sleeve.

I love the way you didn't pause,
dropped everything,
and off.

Grandfather Once Removed

My grandfather, or the man who replaced
my grandfather, lugs home
half a bag of shopping. He is touched
by grief, or something that passes
for grief. Loneliness seems
closest to him as he hugs
the curve of Sandringham Drive,
past all the ways of saying home
to their home, which is more than half empty.

My grandfather, or the man who replaced
my grandfather, opens the door
which opened for him late in life.
Inside are photos of, not hot,
but warm holidays, comfortable
chairs, a thick book where love contains
different definitions. Beyond the blinded window
it is like a proverb, the way the rain
that collects in the barrel will water the garden.

My grandfather, or the man who replaced
my grandfather, moved in with
my grandmother after she was widowed.
He came after her husband,
always,
he came a close second. He provided
a pension, what he knew of passion.
Late in the day they took evening classes,
they grew older together.

My grandmother, or the man who replaced
my grandmother, finally
sets down his shopping. He has been left
until last. He has been left
to spare her the unsparing pain
of this ending. He tries not to wish her
alive. He puts their house in order
and waits for the future to stop
lagging in front of him like an old woman.

Bookcase

Introduction to Economics Introducing
Sociology The Story of Art The Woolworth
Gardener Social Origins of Dictatorship
and Democracy Essential English
for Foreign Students Pride
and Prejudice How to Lie
with Statistics Flower Gardening for
Women A Concise History of
Modern Painting A Shortened Illustrated History of
The Bicycle Two's Company The Last Jews
of Poland Captain Caution A Dictionary
of Symptoms Sunshine Phrase Book Odd
Jobs Household Encyclopaedia Wills
and Probates The Mensa Puzzle Book Macroeconomics

Violins

Overnight, violins appeared
to surround your bed. You had heard
about the prisoners forced to play
through the liquidations, now you heard
their fiddling and you saw when your eyelids
dropped, a man straining to accompany
his mother as she marched with
the other bodies to the end of the line,
everybody marching because
they had nowhere to run; you were in hiding
while this was going on.
                    You survived the war
for forty years until your strung-out
dying, then violins appeared
to screech your name: 'Ludwick!'
Gran would shake you out of it:
'You're having that dream again.'

Plaque

THE ENORMITY OF THE PLAQUE IS CONTAINED
IN A FEW MEASURED CENTIMETRES. IT WAS ADDED
TO THE OLD SCHOOL AT THE BEGINNING OF THE NEW
MILLENNIUM. IT RECORDS HOW THE BUILDING WAS CLEARED.
THE PILLARS GO ON CRUMBLING. THE TREES CONTINUE
THEIR ELEGANT LEANING THOUGH 'FILLES',
SET IN STONE ABOVE THE DOOR, HAS BECOME A MEMORIAL.

THE PLAQUE BRINGS THE OLD GIRLS TO LIFE IN THE PLETZL.
I GRASP THE GATES THAT CLOSED BEHIND THEM.

11 April 2009 *SWASTIKAS WERE DAUBED ON THE SITE OF THE CAMP THEY
WERE TAKEN TO AT DRANCY.*

Portrait of the Magenheims

My tiny great grandfather and
my tiny great grandmother are buried
in this frame—faces without bodies
or first names—Dad can't remember them.
Her eye is an apple for her son.
Her breast is furred. At her right hand, ready
for war, is her decorated husband.
They were shot—maybe they were captured
in close-up first, their shorn heads raised
for the camera's quick scrutiny.

In another time, in another country,
they are surrounded by children,
we were born hanging on
to their strong hair and cheekbones.
I have an eye for my great grandmother—
she sits in the finery of my lashes,
and an eye for my great grandfather—
his snatched medals shine. They have been dead
so long; by now they would be long dead
anyway. They lie behind my dark eyes.

Gran's Pantry

After she died, everything in Gran's pantry
turned to leftovers. The calendar on the back of the door
stuck at December. The light bulb popped,
unable to take the darkness in the room.
Her husband lived like a bird off the last of their food,
he thought he might die when he came to the end tin.
Nothing touched the grief gnawing at him
for the second time in his life. The first time
it was his mother who had gone.

Gran's pantry was the smallest part
of their house. It was a lady's portion.
It was a crumb brushed away
under the stairs. Its sealed jars were full of war,
they were up to their necks in dripping,
RSVP-ing, stiff-upper-lipping.
They had been left standing
like the pillars of a toppled empire.

When she was alive, you could have eaten
your dinner off the floor of the pantry.
Now it was covered in eggshells,
they cut his slippered feet
when he walked into the space
she had left behind her. It was huge.
This room was the preserve of his wife
and his mother.

After he died, following the will,
we raided Gran's pantry
and dug up the cake tin.
Inside was the hem of a coarse skirt
he could never let go.
It was puffed up like pastry
with diamonds.
They were the remains
of a fortune. The real jewels
had brought his mother back
from the camp a lifetime before,
they had changed
in the guards' greased hands
to leftovers—a little bread,
a precious little, some fruit.

Naturalization

Ludwick named the new house 'Leopolis'.
When he first moved in, the garden stretched endlessly
towards home, across the sea.

The small rooms stood
for the huge rooms he dreamed about
going back to, taking his wife and his child.

The letter had arrived from his parents
and lay beyond reach by the silver jug.
He filled his son's head with Polish fairy-stories.

It was nineteen-forty one. The war was far
from over. Later Ludwick dropped 'Leopolis'
and settled for Horner Crescent.

On the eighth November nineteen-forty-seven
he became a changed man.
Albert J Peace of Bank Chambers, Batley

witnessed Mr Richard Woodford
(formerly Ludwick Magenheim)
guided by Gran, absolutely renounce his own name.

Extract

You were sitting at pains
in an easy chair, your hands
pushing themselves forward
in a series of jerky movements,
in a relinquished corner
of the room, a desk-light
was angled towards the wall.
I asked you all the questions
I could think of
but you had only one comment to add
to the end of your life story,
I would press it into the appendix now
before commending you to heaven:
'I don't feel like myself anymore,'
you whispered, your voice breaking
it to me, that the man
I had come to see
had already left the building,
leaving behind your anonymous figure.
I would leave you like that,
the desk-light angled
towards the wall, your words
making angels prick up their wings.

Memento Mori

The flame stands
for all your flown birthdays,
gilding your cake
with a fire the smallest
breath could smother.
Now it takes all your strength
to blow your wish. The day loses
some of its sparkle. I glimpse
how much dark one candle
can leave
before the nurse
clicks on the light.

After You

Tomorrow and the next day,
and the day after that, are early days,
cut and dried on the chopping board
into child-sized pieces. Picking a hymn,
slotting you into the local 'and deaths',
like a last supper you'd have helped to prepare
if only you'd known.
Your blade cutting through the skin like a bit of common sense,
'You have to get on with things, you have to eat,' and
passing round your chopping board: 'After You.'
After You. After You.

Trailer

Dad has always driven slowly
as though he has always been
dragging this trailer, full of loose ends
from his childhood that he can't
let go. The trailer follows the car
at a jaunty angle, when Mum isn't looking
over her shoulder, the trailer turns
into Gran, hanging on
to the bumper, her head down, her wings raised
like a Rolls Royce angel's,
when Mum looks back she will see
just the trailer and the last of the boxes.

Dad sticks to the back lanes
of his childhood, crawling along as though he is
crawling through treacle. He is speeding
in a bicycle lane when the police
catch up. They don't see Gran
or Dad or Mum, just an old couple
with a trailer and hurry them on with the trailer
rattling behind like bones or cans
tied to a wedding car. Dad will stop dead eventually,
when Mum follows, all the trailer's loose ends will spill
over into my living room where Gran's clock is
already losing time on the mantelpiece.

My Legs

In tights, my legs remind me
of my mother's. For years I wore
her tights when mine had run out.
My sister light-fingered them too
so someone else's knees and bottom
had usually bagged a pair first.
The waistbands were nicked with nail scissors.
Cat's hair pierced all of our soles.
In tights, my legs could belong
to my mother. They could uncurl
from under me and go and do
her bidding. They could be
her legs that laddered while carrying
me and my brother, pregnancy silver-
lining the sheer denier inside each thigh.
I take comfort like a child
from my own woman's body and the
intimate relationship it shares
with my mother. In tights, my legs could
go on for ever. Each right foot stretches in front of me.

Staying the Night

My mother is curled up
in the bed I have made
for her. All of my demons
are sniffing around. She is baiting them
with the bare bones
of the body she gave me.
She is trying to keep them
from my door. After nights
without sleep, I don't wake

until the click of the immersion
when the darkness is lifted
around my pit. My mother has saluted the sun
and is waiting for me
in the next room. I must remember this
on all the sleepless nights
after she has gone, when I only think
I can hear her, tiptoeing around me
above the everyday traffic.

Grounded

I have drifted back into
my body like a clipped
angel, a slip of a girl
got up in a nightie,
my head has recalled
its place on the pillow
at an ungodly hour.
Your body continues
its long stretch
of sleep but I am
back in the real world
without you. There is
no point dreaming.

Fresco

Uncle Peter talked us through our third cathedral that day,
delivering the word of the guidebook. Christopher strode
through a storm that flickered above the candles and pillars.
I picked out Christopher not by his peeling god-beard or staff
that was sunk into the murk of the river
but by the child he carried so heavily
though it looked like nothing; a bundle of light on his shoulders.

I might have thought of my father then
weighed down by kids and bills and a brush,
my father who wouldn't fly, who bore
the name of the patron saint of travellers.
He would have been at home painting the hall
while I stared at the man painted into a river
who was struggling against the tide, uplifting me
to the beauty of the Florentine Old Master.

Dancing Lesson

Dad waits in the hall
with his two left feet,
Mum runs late
down the stairs,
making the shoes
in her carrier bag
kick up their heels.

They leave the house,
that I left years ago.
Later, my phone call
catches them out
and I remember the secret
Mum let slip,

I think of my parents
spinning under a glitterball
with the whole of the universe
revolving around them.

I imagine an oily third party,
cutting in between them,
to show how a gentleman
would handle my mother,
or a faded Ginger
leading dad on a merry dance

before the refrain of the love song
brings my parents together,
forsaking all others,
they move a little closer and

try out a salsa,
as though either of them
could put a foot wrong.

Lot 927

All afternoon I think of Dad
bidding on my behalf. His old hand
is my right hand; his head is cocked
then shaken in place of mine.
He perches on a dead woman's settee
or piece of Stag or shuffles, tight-fisted,
among the dealers because of me: the way I am
only ever anywhere because of him.
It is my price he keeps under his sodden felt hat.

All afternoon it rains cats and gilt-
faced china dogs while, warm inside,
I picture Dad boxed in
by foxed portraits, old buggers
of sideboards that have been upended
from their fixed positions and carried by caretakers
into the nearly-new century. I am in Dad's hands
which clench at Lot 925, Lot 926 — at Lot 927
I am lifted, like Faye Wray, above the clamouring auction hall.

It is Dad's gesture that counts: his hand raised
above rubies. The bedroom suite is secondary
in my new house — its gentleman's and lady's ''drobes'
have come to stand for him and Mum. I am small
beside them as the bedside table.
The furniture's old-fashioned nuclear family
ghosts the spare room — where I go when I want to sleep
on the other side of the wall from my husband,
my head buried in my childhood's bygone era.

La Donna

The church is not broad enough
to accommodate your figure.
You put your faith in God anyway,
with a shrug of your covered shoulders,
with a wave of your fan. You kneel
before the statue of Our Lady and mutter
a prayer. Behind your back,
the flowers on your dress skim
over your body, bloom
on your arse. A priest
should come running
to take up your fanning. An altar boy
should unfasten your Jesus sandals
and bathe each clay foot. You are older
than you look. You have come this far
after centuries. You have reached this point
with a prayer. I would raise you above
the hollow of your idol. I would praise you
above the shelf life of her candles.

Burden

I sat in the rush hour
cradling a box full of holes,

and sounds and sweet airs
whenever the cab rattled.

The driver didn't ask or look round
maybe it was God come for you, but

when we got to the vet,
'I can't do anything with that' she said.

I dawdled home, wanting to hang out with birds
a little longer, to be admitted to their fold.

In Passing

Maybe it was a pet snapping
at your heels or maybe a stray
tailed you as you trampled
over everything in your path
to the river. Maybe God threw a
curve ball and a dog appeared
to accompany you as you took your last
steps past the still lines of fishermen.
Maybe you meant to make the leap
out of your skin or maybe you
slipped, leaving the river reeling.
The fishermen see the dog sometimes
that you couldn't shake off.
Maybe they're just seeing things.

Suttee Song

A week after your lover's death,
  Buddy was singing. His voice
 hung like a chandelier
    over your worn settee.
The volume was turned up higher
  than the dog, or neighbours' banging.
It was your lover you could hear
  whispering your song. Rave On.

You were drinking. Drug-taking.
  Beyond the hazy world of the flat,
you were chasing your lover's coffin
 —at a distance—accompanied by Buddy.
You were ahead of the bailiff,
  and Co-Op who would have pursued
for an unsettled hearse and trappings. After you
    there was no flowers. No nothing.
Save for the trailing lei of my poem.

Feral

Their bodies are unbroken, with scant fur and jaded eyes.
  They use the gravestones like easy chairs.
A collecting tin provides for them:
  chained to its post, it swallows rain and small coins.
    When I kneel over the remains
        of the poet, something nudges the
            lowered defence of my back.
Their territory extends from the wrought gates of this
      cemetery
  to the broken heart of the Coliseum
 and all the resting-places in-between:
    the squares and roof-tops and unmarked outhouses.

The Runaway Piano
after an installation by Carlos Santos

The piano rolls
   across the floor of the gallery
settling and unsettling
    the groups of tourists.

The piano is on wheels
   like the gap year students
who skate through Park Güell
    on their way waiting tables round the world.

The piano bursts
   into the Moonlight Sonata
with no one sitting over it.
  ¡Visca el piano! There must be someone

    behind the scenes, pulling the strings
     otherwise the piano could go
out on the road. It could throw its hat in
  with the buskers on Plaça Catalunya.

Exchange

He is the Adamest man in the Garden
  holding the bonny branch of his baby above him
where she extends his grasp on fresh air

Raised above the tumbler doves, she
reports back from on high in a baby tongue,
lifting the day with her idioglossia.

High Chair

It is your seat at the extended family table,
   squatting in my parents' back bedroom.
Next to the brand new chair and cot
   and Bugaboo buggy your mother will buy,
 it is a dinosaur. It came from a friend
   at the club. It is Mum's big secret,
  kept in the room your father outgrew,
   where the walls are patterned with Autumn leaves.
    Outside, leaves bud and branches tap the bay window.

Travelling with Isaac

Tired of toys, you play
with your voice —
'*A-ba!*'   '*Ah-ba!*'

I find a couple of words
for you to chew on like 'apple'
and 'auntie' but '*A-ba!*' you insist.

Then I begin to follow —
'*A-ba!*' I reply.
Suddenly we are speaking

to each other and
holding each other
in and outside of conversation

while, outside the car-window,
moo-cows and choo-choos gather.
I want the car to go on for ever.

'How long
before they start to know
what they are saying?' I find myself

saying to your father, and he laughs
and tunes me out with the radio — 'Who knows,
Yada!   *Yada!*'

Twitching with Isaac

After two hundred years, ospreys
nest in Northumberland. A pair
hover on the platform raised
by the Wildlife Trust. The great birds
fly across the horizon like a prophecy.
Their young wait in the wings.
The old tug *The Osprey* is brimming
with tourists. On dry land
the *OspreyScope* magnifies the nest:
a volunteer fine-tunes the lens and tells me
when to look—there is a chick, a flash
of wing before my focus
goes. Isaac is fiddling with the mighty
telescope leg. This boy knows
he is the centre of the universe. Just sitting
on the grass and giggling, he is closer
to the ospreys than any of us.

Engaged

for Martin and Helen

You were calling from Tunisia, from Australia, from Samarkand,
You were calling from a different time zone, from Scarborough
in the sixties where Mum licked Dad's face in a photo booth,

you were leaning on a summit flagpole calling to tell me
you'd arrived. Both of you, roped together, while I stood
alone in your living room holding the receiver like a conch

to my ear. You were calling from a far flung wing
of your house I had no access to. I held the receiver a little longer
after you'd gone, then went to feed your cat.

Finding True Love

True Love is warm and forgiving
in colour, with a single scorch mark
nippling its silk: kids

in the ginnel, playing
with fire have brought this dress
down in price. It falls

from up above into place
all around me. The woman
comes in, with her corsage

of pins. She will fit me
for *True Love*'s
old slipper. Now

I can see myself
in it. Now I can
touch it like his skin.

Condensation

The shapes sparkle in the window
        when I open the curtains
on our first morning in Craythorne Gardens:

  overnight a mermaid, a hoof
and the spread goddess Kundi
    have gathered on the glass.

By the time you get back from B&Q
        —your head full of wiring—
these bodies will have sagged,

    the hoof struck
the sill. I am moved
      to do nothing

    but watch the haul
      of the nets and wonder
at the art that will come from our breathing.

Scan

The screen with my insides on it
is angled towards the bed.
'You've got a little one,' Sister says,
circling the heart—my heart's
joey—lodged in an inside pocket
of my belly. A strip of photos is
taken and filed. I think
of my heart, that has been
seconded—its old iamb
beating in the dark of my chest.
In the bright light of Ward 40,
Sister washes her hands
of me. The box on the form
is ticked: 'Viable Uterine Pregnancy'.

Clipping

September 30 1987. You are a picture
in the *North Wales Echo*, getting drunk
with your roommate Ken and a guy
from another hall whose name you can't remember.
An 'Echo Girl' cuddles up to you for this photo
of freshers' week. You are open-mouthed, still
holding your high note and your beer
after twenty odd years. When I look at you
on your old stamping ground, I see
a rare manatee; a tiger cub briefly
captured. You look through me. I am thirteen.
Nothing can stop you drinking up and drifting off
into Cardiff where your summer is just beginning.
How carelessly you carry our son in your face.
I cannot bear to leave you to your ex-girlfriends
until I think of your mother: folding and unfolding
the clipping you sent home between lectures
before tucking it away with your childhood
cards in her heart's solid dresser.

Sonograph Story

Before you were born, before
you had a sex, I lay
while the sonographer smoothed gel
on my stomach: 'Come on baby,'
she urged the monitor,
whose picture was snowy.
I coughed when she asked and turned
onto my other side, my heart side,
towards your father, perched
by the clinical bed. Once upon a time—
decades before this appointment—
I woke my parents with a story:
'It snowed and it snowed and
it snowed'. Overnight I could read.
My voice filled their bedroom
with weather—picture-book flakes, the sort
that fly by a handful of times
in a lifetime. It was this snow
that gathered on the monitor, blanketing
your head. 'Hello baby,' said the sonographer
then pointed to your hand, your bottom,
your foot. As she spoke each part of you
took shape in front of me.

Homecoming

There were fireworks all over the city
when you came home. I was Saint Agatha
offering you my breast on a plate.
Your nappies ran green as the grapes
your father was washing, all but peeling
and popping in my mouth. Your cry rang out
the old year. It was the eve of the new,
your first night back. Nothing but good
could happen over our threshold.

Three days later, the radio reported a party
still going on in the highest
pub in Britain—The Tan Hill Inn.
Fresh snowfall was holding the revellers
in suspended celebration. Sat up in the early hours
of your life, we were in tune
with the remote gathering—maintaining
our crackly connection to the outside world
beyond the primary world of the nursery.

Arbour

I can see through the open roof

and through the wrought bars

that ring my body

in this cage without doors where

I am free to come and coo

to come and go

to hang with the tumbler doves

or take off

from this hoopla which

unfolds all around me and

lands like the landed skirts of the Duchy

among rills and soft apples:

there is no ceiling

on the arbour's head-space

its enormity is cast like a poem

out of thin air and metal.

Bait Shed

He was a Whittle man
now he collects logs and lights
the tree house fire each morning
and cleans up rubbish and does odd jobs
and learns a bit
about gardening as part of a government scheme.

Had my Grandfather lived
he would have taken his breaks
with this man, sitting
shoulder to shoulder in the pit
of the bait shed
which in the olden days was full of apples.

Whittle, a former British Coal mine in Northumberland closed
in 1997

The Blackie Boy Roundabout

Standing in place of the pub where the pitmen drank,
The Blackie Boy Roundabout
— solid, dependable as my grandfather —
holds its own in the clamour
of traffic, above the mined earth's
cut and pillar. It is a stone wreath
laid to rest in the rush hour. It is a flat cap thrown
down by a hewer or a wailer at the end
of the working day.

Summer Cold

Today is so perfect, I am almost
living in the present, at the same time
I am noticing your face

has its history, separate
from mine. Your forehead has nearly
been crossed out by lines.

You are coughing in spite
of the weather, you say it is just
a summer cold. I want to catch

the things you are saying,
I want to keep you
with me in the heat

of this moment—as though
we could sit out winter
here in your garden, sipping

bitter lemon which will taste,
after today, like this time
with you, bottled. Our chairs are

temporary, they will fold at the
first sign of bad weather.
Already, a cold

is coming between you
and the sun and
the days that are coming

will get colder than
this one but I can
handle summer with you

under the harshest conditions.
Forget about winter.
Leave it to me.

The Tree

When I raise my foot
off the ground, in line
with all the other women
and the couple of men,
I am expressing myself
simply as a woman
with a raised foot.
When I raise my hands
above my head, they are
swept up in a movement
of hands: of wrists and
of fingers. I hold
my position on an un
equal footing in the yoga
group. At the far
corner of the room, shoes
cool their heels, our coats
are left hanging
while we turn — in our minds'
eyes — into trees. We are
posturing as a forest
together though December hard-
hits the window, our right
knees are unbending, our green
fingers are budding. The odd
rumble from a trunk, a
tumbling foot reveals
the beauty of this spot.
We are only human, it is
written all over our faces.
As a tree, I make a

good woman standing
on one leg. I know
what I must look like
and I'm happy with that.